Michel
de la BARRE

(ca. 1674 – ca. 1744)

Suite No. 9 from "Deuxième Livre"
for Descant (Soprano) Recorder and Basso continuo
G Major / Sol majeur / G-Dur

Edited by
Manfredo Zimmermann

DOWANI International

Preface

The music publishing company DOWANI is constantly expanding its library of music for the recorder. Manfredo Zimmermann, professor of recorder at the Wuppertal Musikhochschule and a specialist in early music, has edited and recorded this Suite No. 9 in G Major from Michel de la Barre's *Deuxième Livre* for descant (soprano) recorder and basso continuo. It is a short suite in the French style with an extended and highly gratifying chaconne.

The CD opens with the concert version of each movement. After tuning your instrument (Track 1), the musical work can begin. Your first practice session should be in the slow tempo. If your stereo system is equipped with a balance control, you can, by turning the control, smoothly blend either the recorder or the harpsichord accompaniment into the foreground. The recorder, however, will always remains audible – even if very quietly – as a guide. In the middle position, both instruments can be heard at the same volume. If you do not have a balance control, you can listen to the solo instrument on one loudspeaker and to

the harpsichord on the other. Having mastered the piece at slow tempo, you can practice the second and third movements at medium tempo. We have omitted the medium tempo for the first movement, which is already relatively slow in the original. Now you can play the piece with accompaniment at the original tempo. At the medium and original tempos, the continuo accompaniment can be heard on both channels (without recorder) in stereo quality. All of the versions were recorded live. The names of the musicians are listed on the last page of this volume; further information can be found in the Internet at www.dowani.com.

We wish you lots of fun playing from our *DOWANI 3 Tempi Play Along* editions and hope that your musicality and diligence will enable you to play the concert version as soon as possible. Our goal is to give you the essential conditions for effective practicing through motivation, enjoyment and fun.

Your DOWANI Team

Avant-propos

Les éditions DOWANI élargissent constamment leur répertoire pour flûte à bec. Manfredo Zimmermann, professeur de flûte à bec au Conservatoire Supérieur de Wuppertal et spécialiste dans le domaine de la musique ancienne, a édité et enregistré cette suite N° 9 extraite du "Deuxième Livre" pour flûte à bec soprano et basse continue en Sol majeur de Michel de la Barre. Il s'agit d'une suite brève en style français comprenant entre autres une longue chaconne très enjouée.

Le CD vous permettra d'entendre d'abord la version de concert de chaque mouvement. Après avoir accordé votre instrument (plage

N° 1), vous pourrez commencer le travail musical. Le premier contact avec le morceau devrait se faire à un tempo lent. Si votre chaîne hi-fi dispose d'un réglage de balance, vous pouvez l'utiliser pour mettre au premier plan soit la flûte à bec, soit l'accompagnement au clavecin. La flûte à bec restera cependant toujours audible très doucement à l'arrière-plan. En équilibrant la balance, vous entendrez les deux instruments à volume égal. Si vous ne disposez pas de réglage de balance, vous entendrez l'instrument soliste sur un des haut-parleurs et le clavecin sur l'autre. Après avoir étudié le morceau à un tempo lent, vous pourrez ensuite travailler les 2ème et 3ème mouvements à un tempo modéré (seulement avec l'accompagnement de la basse continue). Le 1er mouvement n'est pas proposé dans un tempo modéré, car son tempo original est déjà relativement lent. Vous pourrez ensuite jouer directement le tempo original. Dans ces deux tempos vous entendrez l'accompagnement de la basse continue sur les deux canaux en stéréo (sans la partie de flûte à bec). Toutes les versions ont été enregistrées en direct. Vous trouverez les noms des artistes qui ont participé aux enregistrements sur la dernière page de cette édition ; pour obtenir plus

de renseignements, veuillez consulter notre site Internet : www.dowani.com.

Nous vous souhaitons beaucoup de plaisir à faire de la musique avec la collection *DOWANI 3 Tempi Play Along* et nous espérons que votre musicalité et votre application vous amèneront aussi rapidement que possible à la version de concert. Notre but est de vous offrir les bases nécessaires pour un travail efficace par la motivation et le plaisir.

Les Éditions DOWANI

Vorwort

Der Musikverlag DOWANI erweitert sein Repertoire für Blockflöte ständig. Manfredo Zimmermann, Professor für Blockflöte an der Musikhochschule Wuppertal und Spezialist für Alte Musik, hat die vorliegende Suite Nr. 9 aus dem „Deuxième Livre" für Sopranblockflöte und Basso continuo in G-Dur von Michel de la Barre herausgegeben und eingespielt. Es handelt sich um eine kurze Suite im typisch französischen Stil mit einer ausgedehnten und sehr musikantischen Chaconne.

Auf der CD können Sie zuerst die Konzertversion eines jeden Satzes anhören. Nach dem Stimmen Ihres Instrumentes (Track 1) kann die musikalische Arbeit beginnen. Ihr erster Übe-Kontakt mit dem Stück sollte im langsamen Tempo stattfinden. Wenn Ihre Stereoanlage über einen Balance-Regler verfügt, können Sie durch Drehen des Reglers entweder die Blockflöte oder die Cembalobegleitung stufenlos in den Vordergrund blenden. Die Blockflöte bleibt jedoch immer – wenn auch sehr leise – hörbar. In der Mittelposition erklingen beide Instrumente gleich laut. Falls Sie keinen Balance-Regler haben, hören Sie das Soloinstrument auf dem einen Lautsprecher, das

Cembalo auf dem anderen. Nachdem Sie das Stück im langsamen Tempo einstudiert haben, können Sie den zweiten und dritten Satz auch im mittleren Tempo üben. Beim ersten Satz haben wir auf das mittlere Tempo verzichtet, da er im Original schon relativ langsam ist. Anschließend können Sie sich im Originaltempo begleiten lassen. Die Basso-continuo-Begleitung erklingt im mittleren und originalen Tempo auf beiden Kanälen (ohne Blockflöte) in Stereo-Qualität. Alle eingespielten Versionen wurden live aufgenommen. Die Namen der Künstler finden Sie auf der letzten Seite dieser Ausgabe; ausführlichere Informationen können Sie im Internet unter www.dowani.com nachlesen.

Wir wünschen Ihnen viel Spaß beim Musizieren mit unseren *DOWANI 3 Tempi Play Along*-Ausgaben und hoffen, dass Ihre Musikalität und Ihr Fleiß Sie möglichst bald bis zur Konzertversion führen werden. Unser Ziel ist es, Ihnen durch Motivation, Freude und Spaß die notwendigen Voraussetzungen für effektives Üben zu schaffen.

Ihr DOWANI Team

Suite No. 9

for Descant (Soprano) Recorder and Basso continuo,
G Major / Sol majeur / G-Dur

M. de la Barre (ca. 1674 – ca. 1744)
Continuo Realization: M. Zimmermann

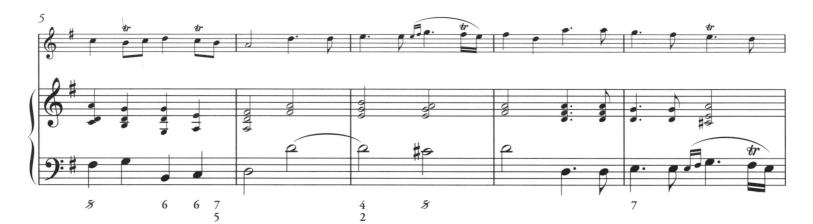

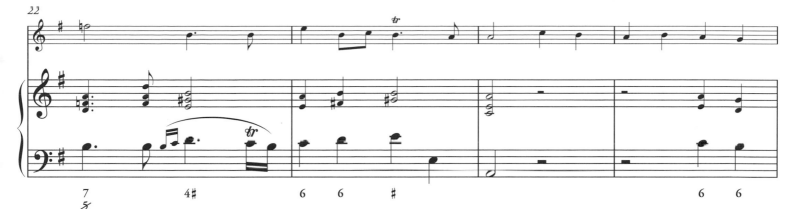

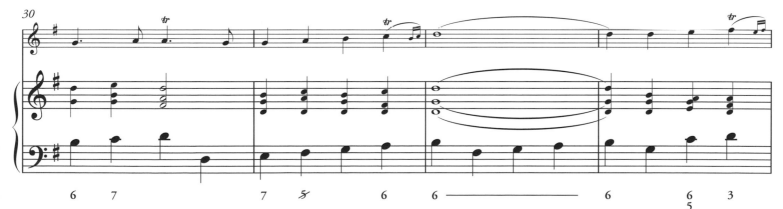

6

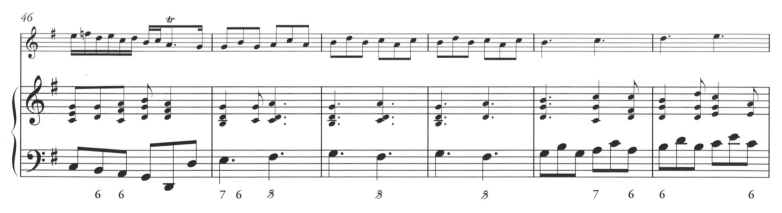

Michel
de la BARRE

(ca. 1674 – ca. 1744)

Suite No. 9 from "Deuxième Livre"
for Descant (Soprano) Recorder and Basso continuo
G Major / Sol majeur / G-Dur

Descant (Soprano) Recorder / Flûte à bec soprano / Sopranblockflöte

DOWANI International

Recorder

Suite No. 9

for Descant (Soprano) Recorder and Basso continuo,
G Major / Sol majeur / G-Dur

I ②

M. de la Barre (ca. 1674 – ca. 1744)

Sonate l'Inconnue

DOW 1501

3

Chaconne

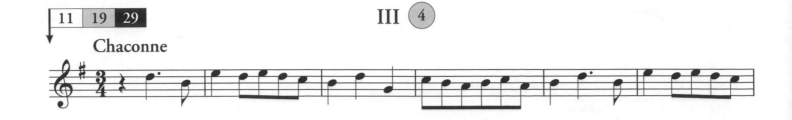

Basso continuo

Suite No. 9

for Descant (Soprano) Recorder and Basso continuo,
G Major / Sol majeur / G-Dur

M. de la Barre (ca. 1674 – ca. 1744)

I

Sonate l'Inconnue

II

Vivement

DOW 1501

(Gravement) ♩. = ♩

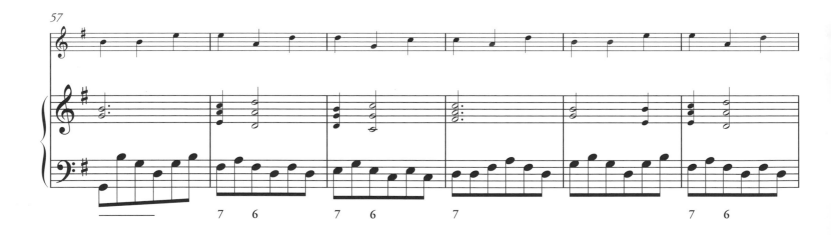

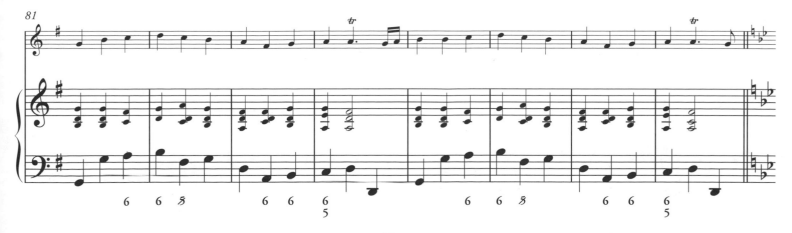

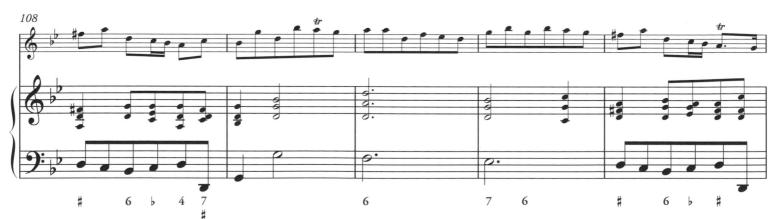

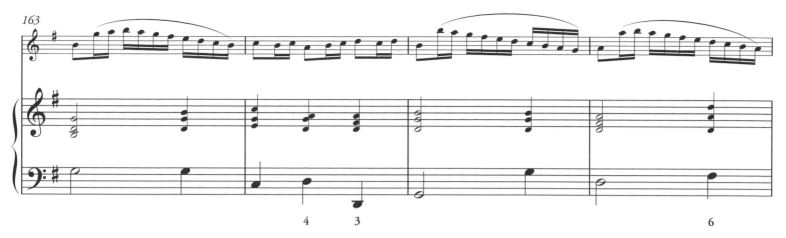

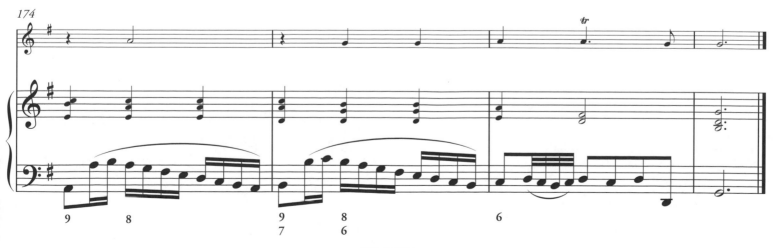

ENGLISH

DOWANI CD:
- Track No. 1
- Track numbers in circles
- Track numbers in squares

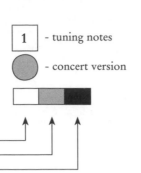

1 - tuning notes

- concert version

- slow Play Along Tempo
- intermediate Play Along Tempo
- original Play Along Tempo

- Additional tracks for longer movements or pieces
- **Concert version:** recorder and basso continuo
- **Slow tempo:** The recorder can be faded in or out by means of the balance control. Channel 1: recorder solo; channel 2: harpsichord accompaniment with recorder in the background; middle position: both channels at the same volume
- **Intermediate tempo:** basso continuo only
- **Original tempo:** basso continuo only

FRANÇAIS

DOWANI CD :
- Plage N° 1
- N° de plage dans un cercle
- N° de plage dans un rectangle

1 - diapason

- version de concert

- tempo lent play along
- tempo moyen play along
- tempo original play along

- Plages supplémentaires pour mouvements ou morceaux longs
- **Version de concert :** flûte à bec et basse continue
- **Tempo lent :** Vous pouvez choisir – en réglant la balance du lecteur CD – entre les versions avec ou sans flûte à bec. 1er canal : flûte à bec solo ; 2nd canal : accompagnement de clavecin avec flûte à bec en fond sonore ; au milieu : les deux canaux au même volume
- **Tempo moyen :** seulement l'accompagnement de la basse continue
- **Tempo original :** seulement l'accompagnement de la basse continue

DEUTSCH

DOWANI CD:
- Track Nr. 1
- Trackangabe im Kreis
- Trackangabe im Rechteck

1 - Stimmtöne

- Konzertversion

- langsames Play Along Tempo
- mittleres Play Along Tempo
- originales Play Along Tempo

- Zusätzliche Tracks bei längeren Sätzen oder Stücken
- **Konzertversion:** Blockflöte und Basso continuo
- **Langsames Tempo:** Blockflöte kann mittels Balance-Regler ein- und ausgeblendet werden. 1. Kanal: Blockflöte solo; 2. Kanal: Cembalobegleitung mit Blockflöte im Hintergrund; Mitte: beide Kanäle in gleicher Lautstärke
- **Mittleres Tempo:** nur Basso continuo
- **Originaltempo:** nur Basso continuo

DOWANI - 3 Tempi Play Along is published by:
DOWANI International Est.
Industriestrasse 24 / Postfach 156, FL-9487 Bendern,
Principality of Liechtenstein
Phone: ++423 370 11 15, Fax ++423 370 19 44
Email: info@dowani.com
www.dowani.com

Recording & Digital Mastering: Wachtmann Musikproduktion, Germany
CD-Production: MediaMotion, The Netherlands
Music Notation: Notensatz Thomas Metzinger, Germany
Design: Atelier Schuster, Austria
Printed by: Zrinski d.d., Croatia
Made in the Principality of Liechtenstein

Concert Version
Manfredo Zimmerman, Descant (Soprano) Recorder
Mechthild Winter, Harpsichord
Steffen Hoffmann, Cello

3 Tempi Accompaniment
Slow:
Mechthild Winter, Harpsichord

Intermediate:
Mechthild Winter, Harpsichord
Steffen Hoffmann, Cello

Original:
Mechthild Winter, Harpsichord
Steffen Hoffmann, Cello